POLE POLE KILIMANJARO

A Little Extraordinary in an
Ordinary Woman's Life

POLE POLE KILIMANJARO

A Little Extraordinary in an Ordinary Woman's Life

BY

SHALINI VERMA

CEO OF PIVOT TECHNOLOGIES

White Falcon
Publishing
www.whitefalconpublishing.com

Pole Pole Kilimanjaro
A little extraordinary in an ordinary woman's life
Shalini Verma

www.whitefalconpublishing.com

All rights reserved
First Edition, 2018
Copyright © 2018 Shalini Verma
Cover design © 2018 by White Falcon Publishing
Cover image © to Cimmaron Singh
Kilimanjaro Trek photos by Ananda Bose

Requests for permission should be addressed to
shaliniverma1@gmail.com

ISBN - 978-93-87193-39-0

**All proceeds from the sale of this book will go to SKILL
Foundation that educates underprivileged children for free.**

The person who will truly surprise you
is 'you'.

Table of Contents

Introduction

Mount Kilimanjaro is no ordinary mountain. Yet it embraces all sorts of people at various fitness levels, and rejects likewise. It is random in its choice of climbers who will make it to the top, those who will enjoy trying, and those who will never make it back. It is elusive at best, and moody at worst. After all, thousands of years ago, it did blow its top to let out all that furious lava. Some of that leftover pent up anger does show up at random. Perhaps it is this randomness that allures us ordinary folks. Kilimanjaro rolls the dice on every climber. Will I make it to the top? Or will I have to accept its verdict and turn back?

No climber can get past Mount Kilimanjaro's intense scrutiny. Standing tall like an intimidating nightclub bouncer, it declares, 'Okay you can go ahead; yes, you too; nope, not you, please turn around; umm, I am not so sure about you but you can hang around for a while.'

And yet, climbers along with their guides and porters will give the climb everything. It's a classic contest between free will and fate.

This book has tried to stay true to my experiences as I along with my six wanderlust stricken buddies tried to negotiate, what to me was undoubtedly a difficult climb.

Each team member brought something unique to the group. Ashwani Balwani was Ballu-on-steroids; a motivator par excellence. Samit Rumde was the wildcard of the group; a complete package of unpredictability and raw talent. Ananda Bose embodied pure empathy and humanity. Karan was royalty; a perfect blend of poise and attention to details. Sandeep Khole was the Dalai Lama; remained pleasantly detached from all the challenges. Ashir Thuyyath displayed his willpower and quiet confidence at all times.

At 5,895 meters Above Mean Sea Level (AMSL), strange things happen to the mind and body. Evidently, I did survive to tell the tale. The tale that started off with irreverence, finally ended as an incredible life lesson of endurance and willpower; a tale that I felt compelled to share.

There were moments of crisis; maybes; I wonder; will I make it; do I have it in me. Then there were moments when life paused a little, laughed a little, cracked up a little, sang and danced a little, and finally rejoiced a little. In the end, it was the journey that was the real hero and not the final summit.

Happy reading folks!

***

The Body

'Are you sick?' asked Simon, studying my face.

I gave him a blank look.

'Are you sick?' Simon asked again, unrelenting and searching assiduously for an answer in my glassy eyes.

His voice seemed to be emanating from somewhere far away or perhaps someone had turned down the volume a little. But I could see him standing just in front of me. I strained my ears to listen intently.

'You need to tell me if you are sick.'

I stood there, shrouded in stoic denial and slowly shook my head.

'Let's keep going,' I said, almost with defiance.

Simon Sam was the guide assigned to my husband and me. Ashir and I had been climbing the summit of Mount Kilimanjaro for almost nine hours through the night. The rest of the group had gone ahead and now were nowhere in sight. The Sun was already out but there was no sign of the summit. The guides say that Mount Kilimanjaro is like a chameleon; you never know when it will change. Even Stella Point, the milestone before the summit, seemed like a distant dream. We had to make it to Stella Point before we could even think about the summit of Mount Kilimanjaro.

I dare not ask Simon how far was Stella Point. It was time to direct the mind to the next step.

I inhaled deeply as though I was drawing water from a deep well. It had to be intense and complete. Then I exhaled quickly, my lungs instantly turning into a pump. I repeated this all over again and silently chanted my mantra, before I could strike my hiking pole in the ground yet again, and earn my next step.

I was two inches closer to the summit of Mount Kilimanjaro.

I had been doing this, often with clockwork precision since we started the climb an hour before midnight. Nine hours later, I was dangerously clinging on to the last few scraps of oxygen in my body. Altitude sickness strikes you unannounced. I had already seen half a dozen people being escorted down the mountain, with blue lips and languid legs, slumped in the arms of the guides. When they gave up, it was absolute and unequivocal.

The sun shone bright, almost too bright across the barren and indifferent mountainside.

Under that glare, I spotted the body, sprawled limp on the ground, eyes shut, and mouth slightly open. I could have sworn I saw him breathing his final breath.

Prepping

A year ago, a bunch of friends found themselves at the base camp of Everest, a moment etched in digital eternity by a Facebook post by my friend Ananda. The seed of my decision to climb Mount Kilimanjaro was silently sown by that flamboyant Shah Rukh Khan style photo that I liked on Facebook.

Figure 1: PC: Ananda Bose's FB page

The same doughty group then set its sights on Mount Kilimanjaro, in the heart of Africa, as their next big challenge. It has the quiet distinction of being the tallest freestanding mountain in the world, and the tallest mountain in Africa. My husband and I became party to the plans and to the WhatsApp group that was promptly created.

Africa has always fascinated me, ever since my dad brought home a book called *King Solomon's Mines*. Today, I feel that the book was a very colonial take on Africa. But it is special because it was the first book I read at the age of seven. Although it was more like the first book my dad read to me. His inimitable style of storytelling fired my imagination about Kukuanaland and the evil old lady Gagool. This coupled with books about seafarer and pirates ensured that I developed a deep-rooted love for travel. Fortunately it all worked out well because my husband and son are intrepid travellers. We have been on the move, but Mount Kilimanjaro was yet to be ticked off the bucket list.

That time had come. Our eclectic group consisted of seven people armed with very different sets of fitness levels, anxieties, and gear.

Samit Rumde - Behind that genial smile was a deep-seated anxiety about man-made arrangements for nature's call during the trek. Absence of that was a deal breaker for him, and most of his efforts had gone into meticulously arranging for a mobile toilet. The mobile toilet was later going to play a huge role in our climb. Winter wasn't his thing, but he believed that whiskey was the all-in-one remedy for all ills of life.

Ashir Thuyyath - Has lived mostly at sea level, but was confident that there is no mountain which he could not climb. He thought planning and prepping were for the meek. He must rely on inner instinct and mind-over-body. He also happens to be my better half.

Ananda Bose - Master planner with a keen eye for details. He took the initiative to turn a shared idea into a well-planned trek. Best equipped with the right kind of gear; complete with a solar charger that would give him nine full phone charges for a 7-day trek. He was all set. His natural curiosity allows him to learn every fact and trivia about any new place he goes to.

Ashwani Balwani - Alias Ballu. The well-meaning happy-go-lucky buddy who always wears a look that seems to suggest that something fantastic has just happened. He was the self appointed minister of keep-the-group-motivated, with his wisdom and fitness. He led from the front.

Karan Singh Kamboj - He knew how to get a good bargain on his gear. He was also the group's official clarifications-in-charge. He ably spoke for the group — the quality of the sleeping bag and tents. He was particularly concerned about how he would fit within the tent. Admittedly, height can be a liability in economy class and tents, something I never have to worry about. His concern about the quality of tents would prove to one of the most important questions we should have asked the guides before starting. Pablo, our trek organiser, assured us about the tents and we chose to trust him. Trust can become a liability in tough terrain.

SK - The dormant one on WhatsApp. Watch this space for more on him, when I actually get to meet him.

Shalini Verma - As for me, I was just trying to keep up with the rest. As I tried to gear up for the trek, I was dealing with three fears:

- Fear of over-packing: I was born with this flaw. On vacations, I pack for floods, earthquake, famine and what not. And this was a whole new unknown tough terrain situation. How does one cram it all within 15 kilos?
- Fear of losing to my husband: I must admit that I spoilt the party for an all male crew. When I learnt that I was the sole female member of the group, I did hesitate. But my husband brushed my apprehensions aside, and motivated me to come along for two reasons — A. Because that's what husbands are meant to do. B. Because he knew that if he made it to the top, and I did not, he could rub it in for the rest of our lives. Losing to my husband was not an option.
- Fear of mortality: The last thing I wanted was an unfortunate departure from this world — my soul taking sudden flight right from the summit of Kilimanjaro. For Mother Nature, the convenience of this whole matter at high altitude can hardly be denied. So I had to plan for any eventuality. I called up my son who is studying in a boarding school, and gave him the main legacy my husband and I would be leaving behind — passwords to everything. Millennials do not need a well-crafted will. Give them your passwords, and they can take it from there. Staying true to his teenage spirit, he seemed more concerned about his education funding than our survival at the summit. I did assure him that I would do my best not to die so that his college funding would be unhindered.

As D-Day neared, the WhatsApp group started to buzz with suggestions on what to buy, how to train, etc., etc. I have to admit that the hardest part of climbing Mount Kilimanjaro was the heavy price you pay gearing up for it. The list of essentials was daunting. My dear friends Anjana and Rahul lent me some gear.

Then my husband and I went on an outrageous shopping spree. We were joined by fellow mountaineer Samit Rumde, who drove down from Abu Dhabi to Dubai, amply supported by his cheerleaders — wife Ashwini and daughter Trisha. I relied entirely on Samit for shopping advice because of the wisdom he had accumulated during his trek to Everest Base Camp. Samit invested in a very fancy solar charger for phones. I was already planning to be best friends with him.

An outdoor store is a window to a whole new parallel universe. Evidently the makers of the gear think through every detail. For everything indoor, there is an outdoor version. For example, the water bottle is not just your average everyday bottle; it is a full scale hiking survival hydration system consisting of a long tube for sipping the water, and a bladder bag for storing water, to be placed in the outer pocket of your backpack. It is popularly called CamelBak, the original creators of such hands-free hydration packs.

Everything in the store looked amazing, weighed nothing, cost everything. With empty pockets and a car full of hiking shoes, hiking pants, hiking jackets, hiking gloves, hiking caps, hiking socks, hiking towel (yes that's correct, you need feather weight microfiber towels), I came to realise that the height of a mountain is directly proportionate to the heavy price you pay when preparing to scale it. Yet the Sherpas hop, skip and jump to Everest in half the gear I had piled up in my spare room. Maya, my lovely domestic help, who hails from Nepal, was half suspecting that my trek was to Mars and not to some mountain summit.

Then came the list of vaccines. Our entire group of climbers grew up in one of the most virus and bacteria friendly lands in the world. Delhi belly is a way of life for foreign travellers to India. It's not a question of whether or not they will fall sick, but when. They all (including the legendary Steve Jobs) come in search of their spiritual self, and return with a belly full of bugs. After all, the body must go through a diarrheal test before the mind can be evolved.

Indians who move overseas surprisingly lose their resistance to Indian bugs in a matter of six months. If you spot an Indian using mineral water while brushing his/her teeth, you know instantly that he/she must have lived outside India for at least six months. Ideally, we should have been fine in Africa without vaccines but traveller clinics instill a definitive fear of the African variant of Typhoid, Tetanus, Diphtheria, Malaria and so forth. The Indian belly was expected to be quite vulnerable in Africa. The yellow fever vaccine is a deal breaker in many African countries. So we could not argue about that. As we walked out of the clinic with all the shots and a stiff arm, we were deemed medically fit for Kilimanjaro.

Dubai is plain wrong for training for a mountain trek. Admittedly, it's rather unfair to expect a desert to take on the responsibility of making us mountain fit. In August, temperatures were still hovering around 40 degrees Celsius even at night, so training outdoors was not going to happen for me. But I had to get the job done one way or the other. I did not want to be the single point of failure for our gutsy group.

10

So I decided to make good use of our two flights of stairs in our villa. I packed ten kilos of dummy gear in my backpack, put on my hiking shoes and started walking up and down the stairs. My initial target was climbing 45 storeys (two flights of stairs = one storey), and then I added another 30, to complete 80 storeys in about an hour.

But my dogs — Razia Sultaan (a South African Boerboel) and Junior Singh (a German Shepherd Dog) were not impressed. They thought, *'She can't quite make up her mind if she wants to stay upstairs or downstairs. All this heat is making her lose her mind.'*

Initially, Razia tried to save me from the madness by accompanying me up and down the stairs. After a few failed attempts to guide me, they just sat at the bottom of the stairs, terribly worried about my mental condition, waiting for the madness to stop.

Figure 2: Is she going crazy?

Meanwhile, the rest of the group in Singapore knew exactly what to do and were doing their weekend treks around the island. They made it look easy. The bonhomie and camaraderie was evident. Their WhatsApp photos motivated me to keep at it.

My husband and I became cut throat competitors with our training regime. Initially, Ashir was lagging behind on his fitness regime. Then on a trip to his hometown in India, he decided to go on a long walk. Five hours later, he had covered 31 km! To me, it amounted to a declaration of war.

You would think that a husband and wife duo going on their first ever trek would make this about teamwork, sharing and caring. Not at all. Failure was not an option. It was each one for him/herself. While I was on a business trip overseas, Ashir was secretly trying to get ahead, doing his 3-hour walks. On my return, when I got wind of it, I cranked up the fitness regime.

By then outdoors had become a bit more hospitable in Dubai. My trial hikes took me around the neighborhood in my hiking boots and my

Figure 3: Ashir's annoying Nike Fuel update in our WhatsApp Group

daypack. The hiking terminologies are important if you want to be part of the group. A backpack taken on a trek is called a 'daypack' with an assortment of your belongings to last you a day. The porters have to carry the rest in a duffle bag.

I strapped on my hiking boots that needed some serious breaking in. This was quite a departure from the cowboys breaking in horses in the 19th century. In the 21st century, climbers need to apply serious technique to break in their hiking boots. I wore them to everyplace I legally could without being thrown out for inappropriate dressing. After a while, Ashir started to mildly protest my fashion malapropism to lunches and dinners in public places.

I was quite a spectacle with my daypack on my back, looking serious and determined like a hawk, making a dash for the imaginary prey. Bewildered neighbors spotted me on a hike to nowhere. The neighborhood watch may have issued a warning on their Facebook group page that a schizophrenic middle aged Indian woman was walking around thinking she was back home in the Himalayas.

Letting Go

Disaster struck in the final week before our flight to Tanzania. On my business trip to Nairobi in the previous week, a gentleman was sniffing ominously during a meeting. I could sense the impending danger. He proudly announced that he had been advised to stay home, but his unstinted devotion to his work motivated him to come to office and put everyone at risk, as he generously spread the flu to every human he came in contact with. I was not able to concentrate on what he was saying — elaboration of attractive business opportunities interspersed with his sniffs and coughs. I think the flu virus could sense fear. My anxiety must be an open invitation to Mr. Virus. He spotted fearful-me sitting across the table, and decided to make its move. By the time I returned, I was sitting with a box of tissues in search of a miracle from medical science.

The massive body of work and innovation in medical science has helped mankind (including but not limited to womankind), survive virulent diseases. But when it comes to common flu, all the medicines recommended by doctors cure your cold in one week if you took those medicines or in seven days if you didn't take them. In such situations, the only relief I get is by having a dose of the unassuming Ginho. No relation to gin and tonic but everything to do with ginger+honey, a magical potion passed down by generations of know-it-all grandmas in India. But I didn't need relief, I needed a quick and dirty cure. So I tried every remedy in the manual of flu remedies.

Finally, when nothing works, you just leave it to the good offices of the higher consciousness aka God. That's what I did; I prayed hard. I am a Hindu by birth, and remained so possibly out of sheer spiritual inertia. I was adequately familiar with the Hindu way of conversing with God, which was a combination of smoky incense sticks offered to God in slo-mo tai chi style, some mantras and a good dose of random conversations. We tend to assume that like modern day software, God is familiar with NLP — Natural Language Processing. If you are not familiar with NLP, then I suggest you familiarize yourself with Artificial Intelligence. If you are in the technology industry and you don't know NLP, then you should quickly abandon that rock you have been living under.

My conversations with God were mostly like a plea bargain as lawyers do during an out-of-court settlement. After some intense negotiations, the deal was made. And now He had to deliver the goods. I tend to think that God is a He. After all, why would the ostrich I spotted in the Nairobi National Park looked like a million bucks, while the lady in his harem looked like his badly done photocopy.

Just days before any vacation, your whole life starts to fall apart. Tenders miraculously appear, which require your immediate attention. You have this feeling that everyone you know and don't know has suddenly developed a strong desire to meet you. Meetings and presentations must be done at the nth hour. Your dogs start to give you that 'look'. You suddenly start to feel like a dotard.

15

Figure 4: No points for guessing who is Mrs. Ostrich

Recently, the North Korean dictator and rocket man felt obliged to question Donald Trump's mental stability by publicly asking him, 'Are you a Dotard...?' This sent half the world (including me) scrambling for dictionary.com, which declared that Dotard is a person, especially an old person, exhibiting a decline in mental faculties; a weak-minded or foolish old person. Pronounced as [doh-terd], though it would have sounded more appropriate as [Doh-Taard]. The word was very fashionable in the early 1800s, after which it fell into disuse. It must have been a lot of hard work for the sidekicks of Kim Jong Un to go all the way back to the 1800s to find a suitable description for a man they love to hate.

While dotard is an unsavoury description of elderly people, it seems rather apt for Donald Trump in the light of his Twitter rants, even if you forgive him for Covfefe-gate. I was now feeling like #DotardTrump. The prospect of seeming loss of control of my regular life because of no access to phone or the Internet was killing me. The only solution to this problem was the powerful concept of delegation. Letting go was the hardest part.

Amidst the prepping mayhem, my mum gave me some life lessons over the phone. She told me not to be too *bahadur*. Normally *bahadur* is a very honorable Hindi word, mostly used to describe brave soldiers. However, when applied to me by my mum, it means 'unnecessary bravado to prove a point and then landing in trouble.' She knows me all too well.

In my life, my mum is in charge of worrying. As any mum, she developed a rich perspective of every possible thing that could go wrong with her daughter going on a trek, i.e. rolling down the mountain and breaking her head, becoming lunch for hungry wild animals, getting bitten by vengeful snakes, or simply getting lost.

What she was really trying to say was — 'Enjoy the journey, and don't be too hung up on quickly reaching the summit.'

Packing was a project in itself. It needed meticulous planning. Everything had to go into a duffle bag and the daypack. I tried to put some method to it. I split my things into three piles:

1. Absolute essentials or life saving,
2. Essentials,
3. Nonessentials (in other words not-needed).

Strangely, we are most attached to the nonessentials. There was little room for glamour in my bags, and I had to undergo a painful process of detachment.

In the final hours before the flight, the process of elimination began. I would pick every item and ask myself, 'Do I really need this? Can I do without it?' Finally this is what I ended up with.

Figure 5: Things that went with me

The 4:00 am alarm went off, and Ashir and I were on our way to one of the biggest adventures of our life.

As we walked across the aerobridge onto the Kenyan Airways plane, the glorious red Sun was rising above the sandy haze in Dubai, giving the city a fresh pink hue, and gently telling us that we were going to be just fine.

At the airport, we had a minor glitch while checking in. The airport staff loved my name so much that she put my name on my boarding pass and on Ashir's boarding pass. Ashir nearly boarded the plane as me. But the matter was spotted and quickly resolved with the necessary apologies tendered. No need for a Twitter rant about crazy airlines.

After boarding, the ceremonial selfie was taken and posted even as the airhostesses kept asking us to turn off all our electronic devices.

Cut to five hours later, we landed in Nairobi on transit. The toilet at the Jomo Kenyatta International Airport had turned wild. The flush in every loo was on an indefinite strike. The janitor casually asked me to dunk the bucket in a drum of soapy water and use that for flush water. Growing up in India, a complete and unequivocal distrust of public toilets was already in my DNA. This was no big deal. As Ashir put it, the Nairobi airport was training me for the impending toilet doom.

The other members of our group were all well on their way to Kilimanjaro. No mishaps reported except for the airline misplacing SK's baggage. But he was unfazed.

While we waited for the final boarding call in Nairobi, our hearts were already in Kilimanjaro. The plane we boarded from Nairobi to Kilimanjaro was called Precision Air. It was a small plane with propellers that instantly transported me back in time by a few decades. The look and feel of the plane inspired little confidence and gave me a feeling that was quite opposite of what its name represented. A quick mental calculation told me that from the current state of the plane, we had a 60% probability of landing safely. I was acutely listening to the safety guidelines. The captain mentioned how we could use our seats as floatation devices, even though the flight path of this plane was nowhere near the ocean. I wished myself safe travels.

At the Gates

We landed in Kilimanjaro without any mishap. The Kilimanjaro airport is very small, just like small town airports in India. Upon landing, you could be in the arrival hall in 15 minutes if you do not need a visa. But we had to tackle a tricky problem at the visa-on-arrival section. It's not very often that Indians enjoy the privilege of visa-on-arrival at airports. So I made sure that we had a copy of every possible document, for a smooth entry. Despite the extreme planning, I couldn't find the pen I had packed in one of the half a dozen pockets of my backpack. Tethered pens, a species of pens commonly found in any immigration section were clearly missing at the Kilimanjaro airport. If you don't have a pen at an immigration or visa counter, you feel like a lost sheep looking around and silently bleating.

By default, all socially awkward tasks such as borrowing a pen from total strangers, become my responsibility. Ashir looked blissfully detached. So I had to quickly get into action. I walked up to the visa counter to make my formal plea for a writing tool. I got a curt 'No'. The angry look on the visa officer's face said, '*Go get your own pen, if you want to enter this country.*' Great! We were supposed to import pens to apply for a visa. The other option was to borrow a pen from a willing passenger. I scanned the area for the friendliest looking passenger who had completed his scribbling project. I spotted an elderly person who seemed least likely to reject my request. I made my move.

'Could I borrow your pen please?'

The kind-hearted soul happily handed the pen to me. I now had to scrawl faster than the speed at which he would get to the visa counter, procure his visa and reach the immigration counter. The race was on and pressure intense.

In some countries, the person designing an immigration card or avisa application form has mastered the art of capturing maximum information in the smallest piece of paper real estate. The Tanzanian arrival form is fairly easy except that it is trilingual — English, Swahili and French. You have to train your eyes to spot the words you truly understand. But there was none of the first world declaration requirements such as I-am-bringing fruits, vegetables, seeds, insects, disease agents or soil. No requests for declaring smuggled snails, as made by the US Customs Declaration Form, which doesn't seem to care as much about smuggled firearms. One would think that the snail lobby is even stronger than the gun lobby in the US. Or admitting to your recent escapade to Africa, a major concern for Australian immigration. In Africa, thankfully they have no such anxieties.

Accordingly to my family tradition, I have been bequeathed the honor of filling in forms for everyone. And so I did — with a combination of great speed and illegible handwriting. During that sincere mayhem of getting every word in, the owner of the pen had advanced to immigration, and was looking as stressed as I was.

I had to get through all the information that the Tanzanian government was possibly never going to look at or ever decipher. The form asks you the purpose of visit. In my history of travels to foreign lands, this was the only visa application, where I wrote 'Climb a mountain' as my purpose of visit. What else do foreigners fly into Kilimanjaro airport for? I managed to return the pen in time to its very relieved owner.

Outside, we found the hotel's taxi driver, who drove us to Keys Hotel in a quaint little town called Moshi, where we finally met our group of six friends. The mystery of SK or Sandeep Khole was finally solved. We were formally introduced to both Sandeep and Karan in person. The others — Ananda, Ashwani and Samit — have been friends with us for years. It was a warm feeling to be finally part of a group. We were now bound by our unspoken pact to try and climb the highest mountain in Africa.

At dinner, our guides dropped in and introduced us to the extended group, which included two Australian men with their respective daughters and three Bulgarian girls from London.

Godfrey Said Mafole, the head guide, drew the trail on a blank sheet of paper. He laid out the overall plan that included the route and the campsites we would stop at. There was a degree of fuzziness in this plan.

'We will see. When we get to the campsite, we will make our plan.'

He seemed to have consciously honed his leadership skills. He spoke with purpose and firmness, and smiled sparingly, but he was gentle in his approach. Nicolaus or Nick was the assistant guide who would later be a key source of support and advice. The hierarchy and roles were carefully adhered to.

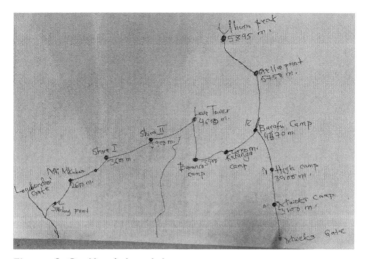

Figure 6: Godfrey's hand drawn map

The guides inspected our gear and clothes to be certain that we were well prepared for all the climatic zones on Kilimanjaro that started in the rainforest and ended up in the arctic desert. To think that in the next six days, we were going to go through a microcosm of what our planet represents.

Next morning, more than 40 of us — guides, porters, climbers included — were stuffed in a 20-seater bus. The minibus slowly made its way through a very green town of Moshi. The roads were lined with trees, cottages and farms growing banana, coffee beans, and vegetable. We were headed to an entry gate of Mount Kilimanjaro Park.

At the Londorossi Gate, I felt like I was transported back to a bazaar in India. Guides, porters, job seeking freelance porters, and aspiring climbers thronged the place. Climbers had to enter their particulars in a register. After lunch, we eagerly waited to board our minibus that would take us to the start of the Lemosho route. The porters' bags could not weigh more than the mandated 20 kg — 15 kg allocated for our things and rest for theirs. This is why it was very important for us to pack responsibly. Every gram counts at higher altitudes.

The porters were made to stand with their bags in a line formation as though they were part of an infantry unit. All the bags were diligently weighed on a large weighing machine. After some meticulous planning and intense discussion, followed by loading, unloading and reloading by the porters, we were bundled into our minibus, as the driver drove us to the Lemosho trailhead. We had an auspicious start, as cans of juice started to rain down on us from both sides of the minibus. When we alerted the guides that something was leaking from the bags on the rooftop, they glanced up and remained unperturbed. It was business as usual.

'No juice for dinner tonight,' someone muttered.

Relative to other routes to Mount Kilimanjaro, the Lemosho route is a longer climb, covered over 6–8 days. The 70-km trail is considered the most scenic route, and credited with one of the highest success rates for summit climb. It starts at an altitude of 2,100 meters AMSL from the western side of the mountain, circling around the mountain through the rainforest, going up to the Shira ridge, and then cutting across the Moorland on the Shira plateau. Shira was one of the three volcanic peaks of Kilimanjaro, which subsequently collapsed — the other two being Kibo and Mawenzi. The trail then veers slightly north towards Lava Tower, and then descends to the Barranco valley. The trail finally hits the Southern Circuit, through the Karanga Valley to Barafu Basecamp, and onwards to the Uhuru Peak along the Kibo crater.

The minibus came to a stop near a small clearing. We got together to take a group photo to mark the start of what promised to be six extraordinary days.

Figure 7: Raring to go

Just like that we got going with our daypack on our back and hiking poles in our hands. The three hours trek covered six km uphill through the rainforest. We spotted a few gorgeous and shy colobus monkeys playing hide and seek through the trees.

The porters and assistant guides raced ahead of us to pitch our tents and cook our dinner. We learnt the 'porter-coming-through' etiquette — our cue to step aside and let the porter pass along the narrow path. I was in awe of the porters racing past us with an assortment of bags of all sizes. There were young porters and elderly porters. They carried everything we needed — our duffle bags, tents, chairs, pots and pans, cooking gas cylinders, and mobile toilet. They wore average sports shoes but walked at tremendous speed. Despite the heavy load they were carrying, they still found time to greet us in Swahili 'Jambo'. Sometimes they would say 'Mambo' (what's up). The default response was 'Poa' (cool), no matter how tired we were.

The walk seemed pretty straightforward, but because we had started late, by the time we arrived at Mti Mkubwa Camp, it was dark and chaotic. There were plenty of people camped there already. The campsite was in the middle of a forest, and felt very cramped with the swarm of people and tents. Our tents were pitched at the far end. The porters were working hard, trying to make us comfortable.

Samit, who was not feeling well because of mouth ulcers, disappeared in the first double tent he spotted. He had to share the tent with Sandeep. But once he was inside the tent, he learnt the inconvenient truth about the limited space to be shared by two grown men. Sandeep just smiled it off. He was the Dalai Lama of our group — unaffected by any inconvenience. The tent could be small, pitched on a slope, the food could be unappetizing — it didn't matter. Sandeep would still be smiling and appear calm. The trek was not just a lesson in acclimatizing to the weather but also to living in tents, to basic amenities, and smiling through it all. On that first night, there was a bit of tent grabbing by some group members who unfairly staked their claim on a certain tent, but eventually everyone learnt to coexist and adjust. As the tent was pitched on a slope, many of the sleeping bags along with its occupant gradually travelled in the night to one end of the tent. We managed to sleep through this as well.

***

Of Airy Tents, Piku and Pole Pole

We got acquainted with what would become a constant through the entire trek. For one, we were introduced to the nasal orchestra of Ashwani and Ananda at night. It was more like a snoring duet with Ashwani at the drums, while Ananda played the trumpet. Ananda was quick to qualify Ashwani's performance as that of a 'nagara', the traditional war drum that has a thunderous sound. On most nights, I was so tired that I rarely heard Ashwani's Nagara, but he joyfully played it with full gusto.

The second was what Godfrey, the head guide called a 'short briefing'. A motivational speech at dinnertime, which also included guidance on the next day's schedule, what to wear and carry, etc., etc. Then Nick, the next in command, would produce a finger pulse oximeter that measured our oxygen level and heart rate. It was the only scientific measure or our moment of truth about our medical fitness at high altitudes. But the contraption was somewhat moody. On most nights, it picked on at least one person and got its reading really wrong. By wrong I mean, the pulse rate reading was so low that the climber in question would start to question his/her very existence on planet earth. This happened to me a couple of times, but I was pretty confident that I was not dead. It happened to Ashwani who, judging by his energy levels, couldn't have been walking dead. After a couple of attempts, the oximeter would start to behave itself. But this was pretty scary because we could never really be sure. Ashir had his moment of scare when he got a pulse rate reading of 42. That time, the oximeter stubbornly stood by its reading, which ensured that Ashir never again experimented with his water intake. The only person the oximeter did not pick on was Sandeep. Our Dalai Lama's heart rate was always perfect because he was the fittest amongst us.

The junior guide was given the onerous task of waking us up at 6:30 am by luring us out of our warm tents with a promise of a bowl of warm water.

'Hello.'

No Answer. Let me pretend that it is a dream.

'Hello. Good Morning.'

Sadly, it was for real.

'Hello,' was my muffled reply from inside my sleeping bag.

'Hot water.'

'Thank you,' I replied sullenly, with my mind screaming, 'Go away!'

Every morning the words 'hot water' would send a chill down my spine. This was pretty much the only hygienic luxury we were entitled to in the morning. If I didn't get out in a timely fashion, the hot water would quickly turn into chilled water.

We needed to be dressed and packed within 30 minutes — getting out of the sleeping bag and manoeuvring inside our tents to wear our clothes was like performing an inelegant version of a classical Indian dance or hatha yoga. Trying to wear my hiking boots was more like doing

Nauka (boat) Asana — lying on my back, my legs up in the air, and both hands tugging at my boots.

By the time we crawled out of the tent, we were panting. I quickly realised that there was nothing exciting about a tent life with my husband; a life, which I had romanticised as a child, thanks to Hollywood. That myth was convincingly broken on the first night at camp. Our tent was far more modest than the travelling tent that the late Libyan Dictator Muammar Gaddafi had pitched on an estate owned by Donald Trump after Gaddafi's request to pitch his tent in Central Park was politely turned down.

Being small was a significant advantage inside the tent, but not so when I was outside, because my not-so-small husband assigned all tent related errands to me. I spent a large part of the morning on all fours, crawling in and out of the tent. Yet we were hardly entitled to complain because we had a double tent, which thankfully had a double layer. This could not be said about the single tents, which had a single layer and were charmingly ventilated on two sides.

Pablo, our well meaning but profit conscious trek-in-charge, must have bought these low cost summer tents on Ebay. He either missed the small print about the tents being fit for beaches in his home country Brazil, or thought that nature had equipped climbers with thick insulated bear hides. At 3,500 meters AMSL, beach tents were a bit of an anachronism. Even the Aussie and Bulgarian brigade, generally accustomed to living in colder climes, was not impressed by the beach tents.

Over the past 100 years, global warming has destroyed more than 80% of the glacial ice on Mount Kilimanjaro (further accelerated by the meltdown of Trump government's climate change policy), yet the sliver of snow on the summit did not merit beach tents. After a couple of sleepless cold nights, the single tent occupants revolted and demanded better tents. The guides got the point and sent an emissary to Moshi to fetch better tents.

Figure 8: Airy tent for two

In our group, the victims of the airy tents were Sandeep, Samit, and Karan. At every campsite during our climb, they held on to the hope of seeing 'better tents'. Just as we were beginning to think that the 'better tents' were unicorns, they arrived at the second last campsite. Brave porters walked all day through a shorter route to get us the tents. Sandeep and Samit got to share the new tent, while Karan managed to remain solo given his height. Samit and Sandeep were extremely pleased that they had a warm tent. Once they were snug inside their sleeping bags, a gust of wind blew the top layer of their tent and they were back on the Brazilian beaches. Warm tents were not scripted in their destiny.

We didn't shower for an entire week. If wet wip
not invented, we could have perished in the mc
at the hands of a skin disease. Okay, maybe that is an
exaggeration, but we sure would have been miserable and
smelly. Deodorant and wet wipes led us to imagine that
we were fresh.

The group members had varied levels of hygiene. On
a scale of 1 to 10, Karan scored the highest. He looked
fresh as though he had just gotten out of a leisurely spa.
Not a hair out of place. Karan was the royalty in our
group. He was organised, alert and always asked the right
questions. He had raised his concerns about the quality
of the tents in our WhatsApp group chat, even before we
had arrived Moshi. He would put his point across with
firmness and without ever raising his voice, and everyone
listened.

Sandeep too looked sharp and professional. Ashir
scored the lowest because of his fear of the cold. This
condition is called frigophobia. According to Wikipedia, this
disorder has been linked to other psychological disorders
such as hypochondriasis. Convincing him to change his
clothes was like motivating the Queen of England to give
up her crown. It was simply outrageous. The only change
he could entertain was adding more layers to what he was
already wearing.

I had to engage in a nuclear war with my matted hair
every morning — the most frustrating 20 minutes of my
day. All seven days in the mountains could be safely termed
as bad hair days for me. Beyond 3,000 meters AMSL, the
balaclava became my constant head companion. Other
than the fact that it made me look like a pretentious bank
robber with a poor track record in robberies, it also added
to my hair misery every morning.

We had to follow a set drill every morning. It was a great lesson in time management. When the guide came to wake us up, he took our CamelBak to refill with water from the stream, which was treated with iodine pills handed out by Ashwani. I had a 2-liter CamelBak, while Ashir carried a 3-liter one. This arrangement was not because of any discrimination based on gender or size. Adventure HQ, from where we bought these, had run out of 3-liter CamelBaks. Every morning, CamelBaks had to be stuffed in our daypack, with the hose or the sippy tube pulled out so that we could drink hands free. Everyone else was wise enough to carry a separate water bottle. Ashir and I didn't realise the importance of a spare water bottle, which proved to be a big mistake on the night of the summit climb. Water is the most important weapon against altitude mountain sickness. When in doubt, take a sip.

At 7:00 am, we all gathered for breakfast in the dining tent — the moment of guilt-free carb loading. We no longer worried about calories. The last time I enjoyed that feeling was more than two decades ago. Hot porridge was a constant feature that we grew to accept and even like briefly and eventually hate. Breakfast also included sausages, eggs and toast. We generally tried to avoid uncooked food like fruits and salad. But we couldn't resist the pineapples that are in whole different league in Africa.

After breakfast, Ashwani doled out half a Diamox to every group member to protect us from altitude sickness. Ashwani dispensed the other half of the tablet at dinnertime. We always went to him for medicines, but the medical advice came from another source.

Samit was a walking encyclopedia on medicines even though medicine wasn't his profession. He could rattle off the medical composition of any pill. He could even advise us on the appropriate dosage. He took particular exception to Ashwani's addiction to Combiflam, which Samit believed was very potent because it was composed of, in his exact words, '400 mg of Ibuprofen and 325 mg of Paracetamol.'

The day Ashwani discovered Combiflam, he must have thought that he had discovered the elixir of life. Ashwani popped a Combiflam for every problem he had on the trek. He was perpetually excited. I half-suspected that Combiflam had something to do with it. He would be cheerful at the start of the day, all the way through to the highest point, and would remain upbeat when we reached a new campsite. I am quite sure that he went to bed with a smile. There was something to learn from Ashwani Balwani's unstinted spirit and energy, for which he earned the honorable title of Ballu-on-steroids.

Just as we were ready to leave, we would get into a flurry of activities. Guides checked the weight of our daypack. They helped us put on our gaiters. We got our CamelBaks. The morning ritual also included adding a handsome dose of sunscreen lotion and lip balm that I always carried with me.

Ananda would be trying different things to deal with his acidity that he developed after Day 2, possibly because of the water, while Samit would undoubtedly be with his most important travel companion, the mobile toilet, popularly called Piku during the trek. If you haven't been watching Bollywood movies, chances are you don't know what Piku is. Piku is a movie in which the perennially constipated male protagonist enacted by the illustrious actor Amitabh Bachchan, was obsessed with his bowel movement. His mood and his sense of wellbeing were dependent on his morning bowel movement. When he set off on a road trip with his daughter, his potty chair travelled with him, prominently placed in the car's overhead carrier.

As a kid, I had witnessed my grandfather obsess over his bowel movement, which was by far the most important event for him every day. If he appeared to be in a celebratory mood, the haloed bowel movement must have been a roaring success. The whole family would be relieved. Or else it would be doom and gloom around the house.

Piku proved to be the most important asset for us during our trek, especially in higher altitudes. Many of us had made light of Samit's single point agenda of arranging for Piku, but he had shown tremendous foresight in insisting on a mobile toilet.

On the very first campsite, we realised that there was absolutely no question of using the public toilets at the campsites. If you were brought to the campsite blind folded, you could have sniffed out the public toilet from a radius of 20 yards. I'd rather freeze my butt in the open than die while using those toilets.

We tried going in the open aka 'loos with views', except that the view could also include a sauntering porter, guide or other climbers. The arctic desert terrain at higher altitudes did not help because rocks and boulders became a rare commodity. It was freezing out in the open. At night it could even be dangerous. So Piku became our toilet of choice. Once we gave Piku a try, we realised what an unassuming mobile toilet could mean for climbers in higher altitudes.

A porter called Hendrey was assigned the difficult job of cleaning Piku after each use. I did not really get into the mechanics of the toilet, but I have to say that Hendrey kept it spanking clean. He would never complain or show the slightest hint of inconvenience while doing what is arguably one of the most difficult jobs in the world. At times, someone would leave Piku in a catastrophic condition, unfit for human use thereafter. At that moment, Hendrey was the man of the hour. He almost seemed happy when he was called upon for help. He would step into the toilet with a smile, start humming a Swahili song as he did his cleaning, and step out still smiling like the Buddha. He was possibly one of the most professional persons I have ever had the good fortune of meeting in my life. We all owed our well being to Hendrey.

I firmly believed that obsessing over bowel movement was a national pastime of Indian men above the age 60 years. But I had a new revelation during the Kilimanjaro trek. Put 40-something men in a tent, you would think that they would talk about mid-life crisis, next big challenge, women or worse porn. Wrong. The movie Piku was played out before my eyes over and over again. At breakfast, half the time was devoted to an intense discussion on bowel movement and pee. No one understood why I was mostly in splits listening to the details.

Men consider peeing a carefully honed craft that they take immense pride in. The trajectory, direction, volume, and timing of their pee were pertinent points of discussion. By the time we reached the last campsite, I grew wiser. I learnt, for example, that they took care not to pee against the wind for fear of an icy urinary backlash in the face. These were real issues that could not be glossed over. This may have been a side effect of the Diamox tablets we were taking. Where and how did they pee during the previous night was how the conversation opened at breakfast.

Over time, Samit developed a strong platonic relationship with Piku, given the inordinate amount of time he spent in it every morning. But he was generous enough to give it some space, and waited for others to do their business before he claimed his precious 25 minutes every morning. So just before the day's trek commenced, when everyone else was anxious about what to carry in his or her daypack, Samit would be found inside the Piku, reflecting on life.

The Aussie and Bulgarian brigade were always ready on time. We, i.e. the Indian contingent, were trying to stay true to Indian Standard Time, which is generally a couple of hours behind rest of the world. Indians have a high tolerance for tardiness. It is well understood that we do not arrive on time for business meetings, weddings, parties, and public speeches. We could get offended if our guests arrived at the scheduled time because we may not even be ready in time for our own party. If you are the guest of honor at a public event, and you inconveniently arrive on time, you might as well help out with setting up the stage. Even our trains make every sincere attempt at arriving late, and a quarter of them convincingly succeed in their mission[1].

Finally, it was time to set off in the morning, with the head guide Godfrey leading the way. We would start walking in a single file. The mood in the mornings was generally upbeat. We would walk at a steady pace, enjoying the view and the sense of calm around us. If the guides saw any of us struggling a little, they would gently advise us to walk Pole Pole.

---

[1] A study by the Indian Railways showed that 1 on 4 trains arrived late in India in 2016. http://www.newindianexpress.com/thesundaystandard/2017/apr/30/train-punctuality-halted-a-quarter-short-in-2016-1599289.html

Pole Pole isn't just a trick to climb Kilimanjaro. It is the African ethos. When Nelson Mandela and other anti-Apartheid activists wanted to protest in jail, they opted for the elegant go slow protest. They would perform their jailbird duties, except that it would be very slow. Nothing would get done on time. This is a brilliant non-violent protest, because no one can legally fault you. Pole Pole is a wonderful reminder that everything takes its course in life. I often test Ashir's patience by resorting to Pole Pole when he is sitting in the car, waiting for me to get out of the house and join him.

Some of the people in our extended group took offense to Pole Pole. The Australian and Bulgarian brigade was in a tearing hurry to get to their destination on any day. It was mostly because they had more stamina than us (the Indian contingent). A nation of software developers largely fed on lentils and veggies are less likely to keep up with stakes fed, sports loving climbers, no matter where they come from. Because they mostly trekked ahead of us, we did not get to socialise with them.

We decided not to stress ourselves with trying to keep up with them, mainly because there was no prize for reaching first. We also wanted to enjoy the walk and look out for one another. We took our regular breaks and some irregular ones. Our cue to get started after the break was a polite *twende* (Let's go in Swahili). Over time *twende* earned some measure of disrepute, as no one liked to hear the word.

From Shira Plateau to Barafu

On Day 2, we departed from the Mti Mkubwa Camp towards the Shira plateau. Our target was to cover 17 km, the longest stretch in a single day, stopping at Shira 1 Camp for lunch. The first two hours was an uphill climb towards the Shira plateau. As the rainforest slowly receded behind us, we were trekking in the moorland that covered the Shira ridge.

Figure 9: From L-R Karan, Sandeep, Ashwani, Ananda, Ashir, Samit

Ashir tried to drive everyone over-the-hill by continuously playing 80s Bollywood songs, further intensified by Ashwani's Bluetooth speaker. When we were living in Johannesburg, every morning, I was made to listen to a certain Bollywood song with lyrics, which I half-suspected was written by a loony bot trained to defy logic. All through the song, a dog barked continuously in the background, possibly in protest. I grew to accept this as part of the Ashir package. But his questionable taste in Hindi music was all too new for the rest of the group. Despite repeated polite protests from several group members, he tested their limits. I think some of the group members accelerated their climb, just to escape from the musical horror perpetrated by Ashir.

The trail gently descended into Shira 1 Camp that is located along a tiny stream on the plateau. The only notable fauna in that area was the White Naped Raven that looks like an upsized version of its distant cousin, the crow. After lunch, our trail across the moorland meadows of the Shira plateau was gentle, but refused to end.

Figure 10: Ashir and I having lunch at Shira 1

The 17-km daylong climb completed over 10 hours was brutal, but helped us acclimatise. We ended up at Shira 2 campsite, which sits on the eastern end of the Shira Plateau. For the first time, we got a full view of the Uhuru Peak of Mount Kilimanjaro. At night, we could see the town of Moshi glittering in the valley.

On Day 3, the plan was to climb up to Lava Tower, a volcanic rock outcrop at 4,600 meters AMSL, and then camp at a lower altitude. The Alpine Desert became evident as the tree line started to recede, and rocks and boulders covered with mosses and lichens became more common. Ashir continued to torture the group with his playlist. As I was approaching Lava Tower, for the first time I felt breathless. My heart was thumping, forcing me to slow down. Nevertheless, the promise of a hot lunch at the top was a real draw for us and we made our way to the top of the ridge in good spirits.

The famed monolithic tower of Lava also referred to as Shark's Tooth, sat pretty on top of the ridge. This was our first major test of altitude and a lesson in acclimatization. After lunch, we were allowed to have the proverbial '40 winks' while our CamelBaks were replenished.

The walk from Lava Tower down to the Barranco Base Camp at 3,900 meters AMSL was mostly downhill through a breach in the volcanic rocks. The trail cut through a beautiful stretch of rocky terrain dotted with giant groundsel trees and giant *lobelias*. The Barranco valley is believed to have been created by a landslide 1,00,000 years ago and is sheltered by massive cliffs, allowing the flora to flourish in abundance. We headed down to the river gorge at the base of the Western Breach of Mount Kilimanjaro. Barranco is the Spanish word for a gorge.

At the misty Barranco campsite, Mount Kilimanjaro was in full view, sometimes fleeting amidst wispy clouds, sometimes towering above us with its vast glacial slopes of the Western Breach and the snowy Kibo summit. It suddenly seemed real and within our reach, but nothing could have been further from the truth.

That evening at dinner time, Godfrey's 'short briefing' was mainly about the Barranco Wall, the one-hour steep 300 meters climb up the cliff. We were advised to keep our hiking poles in our daypack because we would need our bare hands to climb the rocks. I instantly turned lady like and grew anxious about my manicured and painted nails, much to the bewilderment of every man in the dining tent. I was finding it very difficult to present a rational or sensible explanation for my anxiety. Just then our well-informed Ananda casually mentioned that the Barranco Wall was also called 'The Wall of Death'. Thereafter, I was more worried about falling off the cliff than my nails. I found it difficult to sleep that night because of my wild imaginations of the Wall of Death.

The next day (Day 4), in the build up to the Barranco Wall climb, I had to psyche myself in Viking warrior style. The Barranco Wall looked imposing and near vertical. We started late as usual. The path up the cliff was very narrow, so there was already a long queue of people trying to make their way up. The vegetation was getting increasingly sparse and we were now just left with bare bones grey and brown rocks. It was an intense climb, giving us little time to look down or think. We just went from rock to rock, scrambling up the cliff, grabbing any part of the rock, and hoping that the rock on which we were stepping was not loose. The safest and easiest way was to follow in the footsteps of the person ahead us.

As long as you have a good pair of hiking boots, the Wall of Death isn't terribly dangerous, barring the one spot that the guides lovingly call Kissing Rock. It was more like hugging rock. The rocky wall jutted out and so we just had to hug it as we stepped precariously on the dubious looking rocks below. For the few seconds we spent getting past Kissing Rock, many of us saw our whole life flash before us but not Samit. He was the star rock climber, and he moved with agility on the rocks like a mountain goat.

Figure 9: Ananda getting past the Kissing Rock

The porters found it difficult to get past us, so they used an alternate route, climbing over huge rocks while carrying their load. That day, there was simply no time or energy for the customary exchange of 'Jambo' greetings. After 90 minutes, we made it to the top, feeling relieved that the toughest part of the day's climb was behind us, or rather below us. We had a certain sense of accomplishment. To top it all, my nails were still intact. The view from the top was breathtaking. The valley had it all but disappeared under the canopy of clouds. Peter, the guide who was carrying Ananda's SLR camera and tasked with taking photos, became very popular.

After a short break, we set off towards the base camp with the beautiful view of the Kibo summit of Mount Kilimanjaro all along. In just a few hours, we would be making our final ascent towards the summit. I wasn't sure if I was excited or nervous or getting a bit sick from the altitude, but my heart was definitely pounding. The trail dropped into the Karanga Valley, and we trekked through valleys and ridges for another four hours, before we made our ascent to the ridge that was home to Barafu, the base camp of Mount Kilimanjaro.

I spotted a couple of climbers who appeared to be disoriented and suffering from altitude sickness, and were being rushed down, accompanied by guides and anxious looking fellow climbers. The suffering of other people does something to your own confidence. It was visible on my face when I reached the Barafu sign post to pose for the customary photograph. The guides started to keep a close eye on me and started to ask me if I was doing okay. Ashir started to give me an occasional pep talk.

There was no time to rest. We had to go another 100 meters up and down,as part of the final acclimatization. The first part seemed like a normal climb as we went from rock to rock. Further up, the entire façade of the mountain was a massive rock at a gradient of about 55 degrees. We had to just walk on it. I had never been more scared through the entire trek. The prospect of falling off the rock seemed very real to me. I just stopped in my tracks and half squatted.

Peter, who was walking ahead of me, said, 'Don't stop. Just keep walking. Just follow me.'

Samit, who seemed absolutely at home on the rock, echoed Peter's words. He assured me that my hiking boots would cling on to the rock. I stood up tentatively and took a step. Sure enough my boots did the job. I took another step and yet another. Karan was not doing too well. We got to the top and rested for a while. A woman, possibly in her 60s, was walking down. She casually told us that she had spent the previous night on the summit in the Kibo crater right at the top, and was heading back. We were awestruck. Ashir who was having trouble at that point was filled hope that if she could spend the night in the crater, the climb was doable. Everyone was looking for some kind of inspiration to carry them through the night of the summit climb.

Bad Day

Barring Sandeep, everyone had a bad day. Samit was the first on the list. He pulled his thigh muscle and suffered from mouth ulcers on Day 2. Godfrey, a tall burly guide with a gentle demeanour, carried Samit's daypack and accompanied him. We called our gentle giant Mr. G so as not to confuse him with the head guide. Mr. G patiently shadowed Samit, whose face gave away the pain and discomfort.

Samit was the wildcard of our group. After he got over his initial troubles, Samit was unstoppable as though his brakes were suddenly dysfunctional. He even became a bit antsy because we were slowing him down. As the group's wildcard, he was hard to predict on any given day, much like the English weather. Samit did not like to be rules-bound. He took his chances and would go to the edge, but he had the prudence to never ever tip over.

Ananda had to battle a protracted problem of acidity, which meant that he couldn't eat well. He was stoic about his troubles and tried to keep his stomach problems under some control. At breakfast he would simply stare at the spread on the table, but would hardly reach out for anything. We were not quite sure what was causing the problem. It could have been the water or the food. It could even have been the Diamox we were taking every day to beat altitude sickness or the iodine tablets we were using to purify the water. Once the guides supplied him with boiled drinking water, he felt much better.

Ashir had his rough day when he stubbornly refused to drink water on his climb down from Lava Tower to the beautiful Barranco campsite. It was my fault because I had placed his CamelBak upside down in his daypack, so it appeared as though there was no more water left in it, but he wouldn't drink from my CamelBak, partly because he was trying to debunk the theory that water was essential for beating altitude sickness, and partly because the advice to drink water came from the wife. Spouses feel an inexplicable innate compulsion to do the opposite of what the other has suggested. This is the immutable reverse-algorithm of marriage. I have tested this algorithm in parking lots, and it works to perfection each time. If I show him an empty lot on the right, he will definitely park on the left.

Karan seemed to experience a mild case of altitude sickness as we reached the Barafu Base Camp. He suddenly became quiet, looked slightly sluggish while we climbed to the High Camp above the base camp. At lunch, he remained in his tent till he had recovered for the final ascent.

Mine happened on the night of the final summit.

The Night of the Final Ascent

At dinner, we nervously waited for Godfrey's briefing. He told us that the temperature at the top could drop to -15 degrees Celsius, so there is a good chance that the sippy tube of our CamelBak would freeze. To keep it from freezing, we were to blow into the tube every time we took a sip. The plan was to walk Pole Pole and take fewer breaks so that we could make good progress in the harsh conditions all the way to Stella Point at the summit. After that, it was an hour's climb to Uhuru Peak, the highest point.

The incredible night was slowly unfolding. The moon had risen with quiet grace, and perched on top of the craggy Mwenzi peak to the east of Uhuru Peak. Night sky was almost lit up with full moon. Ashir was amazed at how massive the moon appeared. He was absolutely right in his observation. The Earth is what the scientists call an oblate spheroid, i.e. fat around the waste. We were pretty much on the equatorial buldge, and very close to the highest point in Africa. This meant that we were several miles closer to the Moon than people elsewhere on the planet. To give you a perspective, we were about 13 miles (4.8 km) closer to the Moon than anyone standing at the North or South Pole. This explained why the full moon seemed so brilliant, and so the moonlit night took on a whole new celestial meaning because we could turnoff our headlamps, and still see the Kilimanjaro summit.

We returned to our tents to take a nap. At exactly 10:00 pm, a soft voice outside the tent gently put an end to our nap. No drama; just a polite 'time to go'. We must have slept for a couple of hours. Some of the group members couldn't sleep at all.

We didn't need to get dressed. Fearing that we would not be ready in time, we had put on all the layers needed for the summit climb before we slept off. Godfrey had advised us to wear whatever we had, because the wind chill could be brutal near the top. Ashir took his words quite literally and wore everything he had brought with him — we lost count of the layers he put on. He was competing for the most-dressed man award on Mount Kilimanjaro. I was really anxious because I was short of a good quality fleece and a windcheater. My down jacket was a hand-me-up from my son, which used to fit him when he was nine years old, and it wasn't fit for -15 degrees Celsius.

We went to the dining tent for some tea and biscuits. I don't think any of us had time for that. We were still trying to get our water and gear in order.

My mind was in state of semi-panic because my hands had swollen up, and were not fitting into my heavy down gloves. My sausage fingers could not go all the way inside the gloves, which meant that my grip on the hiking pole was not great. There was no time for any adjustment. I just had to start off with awkwardly worn gloves. Even in that state of anxiety, I caught sight of the beautiful night.

The full moon was now high above in the October sky, and had cast a magical silver light over the barren yet serene Kilimanjaro. We lined up in a single file behind the head guide. With our headlamps shining, heads bent down, daypack on our back, and hiking poles in hand, we started our slow and orderly march towards the summit.

We crossed the big rock that we had climbed in the afternoon. I could now appreciate the importance of that 100 meters climb we had done earlier during daytime. Had we not walked on that steep rocky façade earlier, we would have found it very difficult to walk at night, not knowing what to expect. Looking up, we had a breathtaking view of the human chain of climbers winding their way up, with their headlamps on, like hundreds of glow-worms riding on a slow moving snake.

Within an hour of negotiating the climb, two things happened. The guide saw me struggling a little, and assigned a guide named Yahya Abdala to carry my daypack. Our CamelBaks started to become dysfunctional with the fast dropping temperature. Every time I felt uncomfortable, I would request for a sip of water and Yahya would rush towards me with my daypack. Now I realised why the makers of the CamelBak called it a hiking survival hydration system. The CamelBak became my lifeline as I was starting to feel tired and disoriented. The altitude combined with the darkness and inadequate sleep was slowly but surely getting to me. Every 15 minutes, I could hear my anxious voice cry out, 'Water! Water!'

The sippy tube of my drinking CamelBak started to freeze, and we were continuously prompted to drink from it and then quickly blow hot air into it to keep the tube from freezing. I missed locking the tube, so very quickly

I was not able to drink from it anymore. Then Ashir started to share his CamelBak with me, and we thought if we kept the tube locked, we could protect his CamelBak from freezing. This was of no use as we ascended the mountain, the tube of his water CamelBak froze as well. I tried to warm the tube with my hands, but it didn't work. We did not have a spare water bottle that we should have carried with us.

I started to pant so hard that people five yards away could have heard me. We made a pit stop for refuelling. The chocolates started to come in handy for us. I remember Ananda asking for it every now and then. It gave us the quick energy to go another 30 yards. We were now in survival mode, and three fundamental life givers that nature had provided for us became critical — oxygen, water and food (in that order). It sounds mundane now, but at 5,000 meters AMSL, these were all that mattered. Suddenly the uncluttered truth about life's simplicity became evident to each of us.

The first time someone sensed that I was having a major problem was Samit, who asked me if I were okay. But I didn't answer, and so he possibly thought that I might not have heard him. Then after another pit stop, Ananda asked me the same question. To care for another, even though he is struggling himself, comes very naturally to Ananda. I have known Ananda for years. He is wired that way. He was struggling as well because I frequently heard him asking the guide assigned to him for something or the other. But he has a heart large enough to look beyond his own needs. Different people reacted differently to the rigors of the increasing altitude. Karan became very quiet just like me.

'Shalini, are you okay?' enquired Ananda.

I heard him but once again I didn't feel like answering. I was either getting disoriented or wasn't quite sure how I was feeling.

Alarm bells rang in Ananda's head.

'Ashir!' He called out. 'Shalini is not answering.'

Ashir was just ahead, and he stopped to wait for me and started to walk behind me. Every five minutes, he would keep reminding me to breathe. I started to slow down, and Ashir and I along with our guides Simon and Yahya started to lag behind the rest of the group.

Ashir started to talk to me like a sports coach would.

'Breathe.'

'What about all those women?' he asked rhetorically. 'They are looking at you to complete this. So you can't quit.'

This had been his constant theme for the past 18 hours when I started to show signs of discomfort. He was referring to all the women who formed my support system, who had been motivating me all along on social media. They included women who have always wanted to 'climb that mountain' but are unable to do it for reasons they have no control over. I couldn't let them down.

Ashir is a man of few words and so what he did for the next few hours was decidedly out of character. He is not given to making casual conversation. On the other hand, I wake up every morning and just take off from where I had left off the previous night. During our tent life over the past few days, I would wake up at 4:30 or 5:00 am and just start talking to Ashir about anything. After 19 years of living with me, he had trained himself to have a conversation with me with a simple 'hmm' trick. To everything I say, hmm is the default response. He has mastered the art of 'hmm-ing' at regular intervals. My 5:00 am monologue interspersed with 'hmm' was brought to my specific attention by many curious group members.

Everyone needs a motivation or a purpose to climb a mountain. Samit had given this some thought. He thought about all the 50 odd porters, assistant guides and guides who were tirelessly working for so many days to build a support system for us to get us to the summit. He was not prepared to let them down. For Ashir, the climb was about testing his willpower. He had put in the least amount of preparation. This was not because of long hours at work. He was still able to make time for his cricket, even on the night before we were meant to fly to Kilimanjaro. He wanted to draw on his deep reserves of willpower to reach the mountaintop. It was a deliberate attempt to prove a point to his self.

At one of my low points during the climb, I sat down heavily and said to Ashir with an air of firmness, 'I think you should walk ahead, and I will go back.'I was afraid that he would tire himself out because I was taking so long to walk. Maybe it wasn't meant to be. Maybe I was not ready. Maybe I would drag Ashir down before he could reach the summit.

All he said was, 'No. You will make it.'

Ashir is very good at simplifying things for himself. If anyone were to look inside his head, they would find a translator, like a piece of software that takes in a complex idea and converts it into simple binaries — yes and no, black and white. There is no place for grey, nuanced or blurred areas in his head. This makes decision making a very simple and quick process.

At that moment I got up and said to myself with a touch of finality, 'Yes, I can do it.' Suddenly, my mind was filled with fresh resolve.

I looked up to see the glow worms of human endeavour fighting fatigue, sleep, doubt, fear, and altitude. The headlamps were still on, and climbers looked like miners, except that they were not reaching for the depths of the earth but for the sky. Death was lurking somewhere in the shadows, waiting to make its move.

I now had to do something extraordinary to pull myself out of the hole. I decided to put to use a couple of tools I had. I have been a longtime yoga practitioner though I do mix it up with running. I have done plenty of Pranayama and I did practice Kapalbhati Pranayama as part of my training for this trek. It consists of deep inhaling and then several rounds of short forceful exhaling. It allows you to pump in oxygen and increase your lung capacity. But that night I made a slight variation.

I would breathe in deeply, and then exhale forcefully just once (round 1) and then repeat this (round 2). I told myself that I would earn my next step ONLY after I completed two rounds of Kapalbhati Pranayama. I would take a step, while I mentally chanted my Guru mantra. When I chant my mantra, deep down I have this inexplicable belief that my Guru is right there with me, guiding me. This routine infused me with energy and strength. It allowed me to become mindful, focus on my breath work, and not think of quitting. Though the step was tiny, it still mattered as a positive reinforcement. I was moving forward.

I did this with a single-minded focus for hours.

Breathe in...breathe out. Breathe in...breathe out. Take a tiny step and chant my mantra. I did it over and over and over again.

The guides had been singing. The Kilimanjaro song was ringing through the mountainside in the chill darkness.

Jambo! Jambo bwana!
Habari gani? Mzuri sana!
Wageni, mwakaribishwa!
Kilimanjaro? Hakuna matata!

Tembea pole pole. Hakuna matata!
Utafika salama. Hakuna matata!
Kunywa maji mengi. Hakuna matata!

Kilimanjaro, Kilimanjaro,
Kilimanjaro, mlima mrefu sana.

Na Mawenzi, na Mawenzi,
Na Mawenzi, mlima mrefu sana.

Ewe nyoka, ewe nyoka!
Ewe nyoka, mbona waninzunguka.

Wanizunguka, wanizunguka
Wanizunguka wataka kunila nyama

Everyone was feeling cold, and getting tired and sleepy. Karan and Sandeep were struggling to stay awake and were briefly dozing off while they were walking. And so the only way to beat that was to sing loudly and cheerfully. This is how the guides kept themselves sharp.

I was getting increasingly delirious. But just when I thought I was about to fade, I would pull myself in and follow my routine. Breathe in...breathe out. Breathe in... breathe out. Take a step and chant my mantra.

Godfrey confronted me.

'Be honest. Are you feeling sick?' he asked questioning my judgment about my condition.

'What do you mean by sick?' I asked him, trying to catch my breath.

Figure 10: Ashir and I taking one step at a time

'Do you have a headache? Are you feeling nauseated or dizzy?'

'I am just very tired,' I replied.

I was quite sure that I had no headache or nausea. But I was definitely dizzy. One of the reasons why Ashir was walking behind me was because he noticed me lurching backwards every now and then, and then trying to steady myself, like a drunken sailor steadying himself at sea. The hiking poles came in very handy to keep me from collapsing.

'Use my headlamp. Yours isn't working well,' Godfrey suggested. He took off my headlamp and placed his on my head.

'I am going up to check on the others. Simon and Yahya are with you. If you are feeling sick, you have to tell Simon.'

He walked away leaving us under the supervision of Simon and Yahya.

We had very little water to drink because our CamelBak tubes were completely frozen. I heard Ashir shouting out for water, and one of the guides shared his bottle of water. We later started to drink directly from the bladder of the CamelBak. We sat down to take a water break, and I lay back and almost nodded off. Simon rushed to me and said, 'Sit up. You cannot lie down.'

Now that my body was in a state of complete disarray, it was time for my mind to act. This is a conscious choice you have to make, but you are not the only one making that choice. This is why the classic debate about individual will versus destiny has not been conclusively resolved.

For any form of success, we need the perfect storm of effort, intent, place, time, and x factor. What is your intent? Is it authentic and for a larger purpose? How much effort did you put in? Was the timing or the weather conducive? Is the place ideal? Did you take the suitable route? Lastly, there is the unknown or the cosmic factor that we cannot comprehend and possibly never will. All these forces must converge to make anything happen.

Martina Navratilova had to be famously rescued before her summit climb. You can certainly not fault a nine-time Wimbledon champion on effort. But the timing was wrong because just a few months ago, she had been diagnosed with breast cancer and her body had become weak because of the radiation she had received.

As we continued to take our baby steps, my mind started to slowly disengage from the body as part of its survival drill. You no longer feel like a composite whole. The Dalai Lama says that if we really wish to help someone in distress, we should resist the temptation of becoming empathetic. Empathy puts us in the shoes of the person, so we start to feel equally distressed, making us incapable of thinking objectively. Instead, we need to develop a bit of distance, and become compassionate.

Nature has given us an incredible tool called the mind. In times of crisis, the mind can defy the very laws of nature that built it. In a bid to survive, the mind starts to take charge of the body, but in a compassionate way, like a friendly guide. The body senses compassion and starts to oblige.

A glimmer of hope rose across the skyline on the far right. A faint line with red and orange hues appeared, and gradually lit up the shroud of clouds that lay around the Mawenzi peak. Slowly a bright yellow ball showed up above the Mawenzi peak bringing cheer to every climber. Never before had we treasured the rising sun so much as a source of celestial energy. It turned things around for many of the climbers in our group, especially those who had been feeling sleepy. But we had a long, long way to go.

Simon stopped and turned around to stare at me.

'Are you sick? Because you are walking very slow. You must walk at normal speed.'

He was trying to tell me that maybe I won't make it. I should reconsider what I was trying to do.

I looked at Simon for a few seconds. Gathering every ounce of energy I had left in my body, I spoke loudly and firmly, 'I am not sick. I am just tired.'

I was not just telling Simon, but also announcing to myself, to the doubt, fear and weakness trying to surge inside me, 'You can't quit. You will do it.' For a brief moment, I was filled with a fresh burst of enthusiasm, which carried me a few steps forward.

Then I needed another round of talking. The best way to drown out the peripheral negative noise was to constantly have a positive conversation with myself. I was constantly talking to myself and to Ashir. He was growing quiet and that meant that he wasn't doing that well either.

'Ashir, are you okay?'

After a few seconds, I would hear a slightly laboured, 'Hmm.'

The final goal post was not in sight; so the only thing important was the next breath and the next step. Focus is key because whatever energy you have left in your body must be directed at that one thing that must be done in that moment. Growing up in a boarding school dorm, I knew how to get on with my studies in the midst of laughter, squeals, banter, and arguments. I had developed mental blinders that I could put on at will. So I used these blinders against Simon's constant questioning; against the despondent look on people who could not make it and were being taken down; against the doubt that was still trying to surge in my head.

Breathe in...breathe out. Breathe in...breathe out. Take a step and chant my mantra.

Breathe in...breathe out. Breathe in...breathe out. Take a step and chant my mantra.

Imagine hours and hours of just training your mind on the next breath and the next step. We had walked for more than nine hours through the night and morning. The screen under our boots, which was frozen in the night, had thawed now, making it harder for us to climb. Even though the light all around was very bright, my vision was somewhat blurred and the voices of people around me seemed muted. My face had swollen up so much that I looked like a really obese version of me. But my mind was still functioning.

I saw something lying on the ground. I strained my eyes to spot a man lying on the ground. I was delirious enough to think that he had just then breathed his last, even though he had been dead for a while. He was an Australian man, possibly in his 30s. He was supposedly asthmatic and sadly died on the spot. Because he was already gone, his body was lying unattended. The others in his group had been sent back to the basecamp. The guides had planned for someone else to come and retrieve his body. It wasn't just the fact that he was just like us and was no longer alive, but also the fact that at that altitude, when you die you immediately become a trivial matter that must wait its turn. The value of the body could suddenly be reduced to that of the volcanic ash and scree all around. I had this crushing sense of the futility of it all.

I hit a wall.

I simply could not go past it. It was an overwhelming and intense feeling of I-can't-do-it that instantly filled my tired lungs. The next step seemed like an eternity away.

At that moment I could just throw it all in and simply turnaround. It would be pretty straightforward from that moment on. Simon was all too eager to take me back.

Beyond the Wall

A little girl, just about three years old, was walking home with her parents after dinner at a restaurant in the hill town of Mussourie in the Garhwali Himalayas. She was tired and sleepy and insisted on being carried up the hill. Her dad was tired as well, and so carrying his well-fed and rather plump daughter was quite literally an uphill task for him. He asked her to walk instead, but she refused to comply. Her mum could see his plight, and decided to side with him in an unusual moment of complete solidarity.

So the little girl used the one potent weapon she had in her kitty — throw several rounds of tantrums. She refused to budge, and just cried, shrieked and sobbed. Her unrelenting parents walked away, and waited in the dark, just out of sight. For a three year old, it was her first real crisis — a moment when she had to make what she thought was a life choice. Standing there alone in the dark on a cold wintery night, she had to choose between waiting indefinitely for something to happen, and doing something about it. She chose to walk.

I was that girl. I have heard this story so many times from my dad in his moments of nostalgia that I can almost remember it. After that incident, I must have quickly forgotten about it but my poor dad could never really get over it, because even to date, he often vividly recalls how my shrieks were echoing in the hills that night. It was possibly my first life lesson that in a time of crisis, the only way is forward that one must take. I believe, as I am told that I never asked to be carried again.

Forty-two years later, I was faced with that choice once again just before the summit of Mount Kilimanjaro. Possibly, the training that my parents gave me on that night in Mussourie came in handy. And I had Ashir with me, standing behind me like a rock, almost blocking the path backwards. But in the end, it was entirely up to me. Only I could help myself. I had to will it. Never mind my worn-out lungs, my blue lips, my blurred vision, my puffy face and hands, my aching legs and back, and my delirious mind. The will had to be wrenched from the bottom of my guts.

... And I walked past the wall.

I saw Simon motioning to Ashir to not say anything and block the view of the dead body from my sight. Simon thought if I saw it, I would panic. I was way past that now. Ashir in his earnestness subtly moved to my left trying to shield me, and I thought to myself, I absolutely cannot let him down. I just kept breathing and walking, and breathing and walking.

It was not long after we walked past the dead body that we finally reached Stella Point. In that instant, we forgot all about it, and even smiled and fist-bumped the visibly relieved guides. To think that I had all but given up just 15 minutes before Stella Point. Will Smith's words were ringing in my head, 'The best things in life are on the other side of terror.' A very excited Ashir was high-fiving and fist-bumping the guides and posing in front of the signpost. Godfrey was waiting there for us. He measured my oxygen level. The reading was 60, so he said that I was good to go towards the summit.

The African guides believed that 'the spirit of the Dead' was still hovering around us. So they were not keen to linger at Stella Point. As we set off toward Uhuru Peak, joyous returning climbers greeted us with you-are-almost-there. It was like oxygen for us. Every returning climber tried to motivate us.

'I was just like you when I was going up. You will make it!'

'The guide had to literally push me up. You are doing great.'

'Well done! You are nearly there!'

A faint smile and a thumbs-up was all I could muster. I did not even have the energy to wipe the layers of caked up snort on my face. At 5,800 meters AMSL, I couldn't care less. One of the guides eventually used a tissue to wipe my face and nose. Vanity had all but gone. To think that just a day ago, I was obsessing over my nails at the Barranco Base Camp.

The climb from Stella Point to Uhuru Peak wasn't steep, but it is still difficult because of low oxygen level. The oxygen level is almost half of that at sea level. I could see the rest of the group ahead now. Sandeep and Karan were hanging in there by a few shreds of willpower. A guide had his hand behind each one's back, gently nudging them forward.It was very reassuring to see them going through the same mind-body game.

Our sights were set on the Uhuru Peak signpost that slowly grew from a tiny speck into the iconic wooden planks that read — CONGRATULATIONS. I had never felt more alive when we met the rest of the group at the Uhuru Peak.

That ecstatic moment — a shared feeling of pure bliss at 5,895 meters AMSL. The Uhuru Peak signpost read — Africa's Highest Point, World's Highest Free-Standing Mountain, One of World's Largest Volcanoes, World Heritage and Wonder of Africa.

I had dreamt of this moment for more than two months when Ashir roped me into his Kilimanjaro plan. On that day, he had stood by me for 10 hours. He could have walked on, because staying back for me had slowed him down and made it even harder for him. Even when I doubted my own ability to go all the way to the top, he had no doubt that I could make it. The cliché 'You are stronger than you think you are' played out in full measure that day. We hugged each other in a cathartic moment of joy, relief and gratitude.

When the referee of a boxing match raises the winning hand, the battered face of the victorious boxer breaks into half a smile, while the puffy eyes can barely give away the pure joy pumping through his heart. All the blows were forgotten in that instant. All seven of us had our hands raised in unison with the guides who had helped us every step of the way.

No one was left behind. That was the most special part of our climb.

Of course the photos had to be taken. As the group converged in front of the signpost, Ashwani generously invited me to sit in the center. I thought warmly about the six fellow-climbers who had made me feel welcome all along, treating me like a buddy. When I lagged behind, which was most of the time, never once did they display the slightest bit of impatience. I, with my unrecognizable puffy face, showing the strain of the past 10 hours, in an oversized windcheater and ski pants, could still manage to pose and smile.

Suddenly all the six men looked rejuvenated as though the 10 gruelling hours had not happened. Sandeep was the Dalai Lama, Karan was royalty, Samit was the wildcard, Ashir was will power, Ananda was all heart, while Ashwani was still Ballu-on-steroids. I was a very happy wannabe.

The photos could hardly capture the momentous feeling, which will stay in our hearts. Yet, the sobering memory of the young man who had lost his life that day was on everyone's mind. Time stood still for us in the15 minutes we were allowed to spend at the top, before the guides started to shepherd us back. The Uhuru Peak is on the southern rim of the Kibo crater. Beyond the rim lay a huge grey expanse of ash and lava covering the crater floor.

Ashir was far more boisterous on his return, now taking lots of photos. I was only too keen to go down because I remembered Godfrey's words that every 100 meters we would feel better. As we descended from Stella Point, the guides took us down, mostly sliding down on the scree, which accelerated our descent. Karan, Ananda and Sandeep were masters of descent, and were able to head back fairly quickly. Ashir and Sandeep were catching up. Ashwani, Samit and I with weak knees were slower. Ashwani was no longer Ballu-on-steroids on his way down. His smile had all but gone and a guide was literally holding him as he was made to slide on the scree. Samit observed that Ashwani looked like a kid who had been naughty at the summit and was being forced to go down against his will. The guides were kind enough to send someone with some juice that gave us the much-needed energy. After four hours, with a few breaks, we all made it back, tired to the very bones.

***

The Spunky vs. Non Spunky Group

Just as I reached my tent with my wobbly knees and sore feet, I was told that we had to leave in an hour's time for the next campsite. The Australian and the Bulgarian contingent were keen to try and go all the way back to the Kilimanjaro park gate or at least get to the Mweka campsite that was nearest to the gate.

This encouraged Samit, Karan and Sandeep to think about joining them. Samit was already vividly dreaming of a hot shower, and a bed with clean sheets. Sitting in the dining tent, while at lunch, we started to explore different options of returning. Samit was even ready to be airlifted if it could get him to the hotel room in Moshiby nighttime. Nick revealed that it would cost us US$6,000 to be evacuated by a helicopter. Samit did a quick mental calculation and thought less than $1,000 per climber. Then Nick gently broke the news that the cost was $6,000 per head, at which point Samit switched back to the idea of joining the Aussies.

I had no such plan. After 14 hours of walking, combined with sleep deprivation (we had walked all night and morning), I was in no mood to walk any further. I just wanted to crawl into my tent, close my eyes and let sleep takeover. Our group of seven people now was divided into two schools of thought. Ananda, Ashwani, Ashir and I wanted to head back to the nearby High Camp at 3,900 AMSL. It was still at least three hours away, but we thought that it seemed more doable than the brutal 5 hours walk to Mweka Camp. These time estimates were at porters' fitness levels.

I joked to Nick, 'If you make me walk all the way to Mweka Camp, I will collapse, and you will have to get an ambulance to carry me down.'

That instantly gave Samit a brilliant idea. Ideas related to evacuation were his particular forte. His foolproof plan consisted of me putting on an act of being extremely unwell and requesting for an evacuation. The guide would call for the rescue ambulance to the nearest rescue point, and the entire group would jump into it, to show their (fake) solidarity and brotherly concern for my (fake) ill condition. I actually nursed the idea for half a minute, and then abandoned it. It seemed too good to be plausible. So we decided just by virtue of an unspoken majority vote that we would opt for the modest plan of going to the nearby campsite. We all went off to our respective tents for a quick recovery nap.

In that time, Samit's dream of a hot shower must have become more vivid, which led him, Karan and Sandeep to form the 'spunky' breakaway faction. After a sincere attempt at convincing us to join them, they confidently sent their duffle bags with porters headed for Mweka Camp, and started early to join the Aussie and Bulgarian climbers.

The non-spunky faction (consisting of Ashir, Ananda, Ashwani and I) started on the slow but steady descent to the nearby campsite. The Alpine Desert started to give way to moorland with heather and wild flowers in shrubs. We could see the rainforest far ahead. We also spotted a little crowd in the distance. Simon told us that a young Chinese girl with blisters on her feet was being rescued.

When we drew near, to my horror, I finally saw what the evacuation mechanism looked like. It was an iron stretcher on which the patient, wrapped inside a sleeping bag, was strapped with a rope. The stretcher was reminiscent of the baggage trolleys pushed by spirited porters (popularly called coolies) at train stations in India. They throw your bags on this trolley, and tie them up in the same manner.

The Kilimanjaro stretcher was a tad more advanced. It had railings on both sides so that the patient would not slide off, and it stood on one motorcycle tire, complete with a motorcycle suspension for a softer landing. When the stretcher was at rest, the hapless patient strapped on it was almost standing at a 60 degrees angle. Six tough porters would run at great speed, carrying the stretcher, which would bounce on the rocky track all the way down, while the patient prayed hard that he or she would not end up with broken bones from the joyride. I later saw an elderly climber hanging on to his cap and his dear life, as he bounced his way down the rocky track on the one-wheel stretcher. Sandeep even saw a couple of porters tripping and rolling down, when they were trying to stop. A Jack and a Jill had to come tumbling down to stop the bouncing stretcher. I thanked my infinite wisdom and stars that I did not latch onto Samit's 'brilliant' plan.

The descent was still hard for us because of lack of rest and an increasingly rocky terrain. I was wondering how the 'spunky' group was faring. I was in awe of their enthusiasm, confidence and stamina to make it all the way down to the gate.The idea of crawling into a tent and crashing kept me going.

The High Camp sometimes referred to as Upper Mweka or Millennium Camp was at 3,800 meters AMSL, nestled in the semi-alpine heath that had grass, fine lichen on giant heather trees, Senecio trees, giant groundsel, Lobelias and red hot pokers. There was a pleasant air about the camp.

As I walked towards my tent, I was puzzled to see Karan standing there, chatting with a guide.

Ashir was grinning at my bewildered look and said, 'They are all here.'

'What happened to them?' I asked.

'Ask Samit.' replied Ashir, still looking amused.

Even the porters standing around couldn't stop laughing. The youngest of the lot was laughing the most.

I called out to Samit a couple of times before I heard a dull 'yeah' from inside a tent. Samit was back with us. The hot shower was not meant to be.

The 'spunky' breakaway faction never made it to Mweka Camp because of some confusion about how far the bus could come in.

Samit had been walking down at astounding speed, driven by the thought of getting to the hotel that same day. He was just unstoppable until he got the bad news that he was not going to the gate. Suddenly our very own Usain Bolt started to feel immense pain in his legs. A disappointed Samit promptly took out his hiking poles and started to painfully hobble to High Camp. Such is the power of the human mind.

The comedy of errors (as Karan put it) also included their separation from all their duffle and sleeping bags, which on the other hand, successfully made it to Mweka Camp. And thus the 'spunky' group minus their bags ended up spending the night with the 'non-spunky' group at High Camp.

That night we slept like babies. No one really heard the sonorous nasal duet of Ananda and Ashwani.

Grand Finale With Picasso's Goat

The next morning after a quick breakfast, we headed towards the final stretch. It was a beautiful stretch surrounded by rich green and moist abundance of trees and giant ferns. The rocky path made it difficult for some of us to walk down because of weak knees, but we journeyed on. Our layers of clothing were gradually coming off.

Ashir had developed a warm attachment to his layers of clothing. He was still wearing the layers that he wore to the summit. At 2,800 meters AMSL, he was still the most-dressed man. Finally, once we reached the Mweka Camp, Ashir started to feel a bit warm. Everyone in the group stood and watched in awe as he peeled off layer after layer of clothing.

We headed towards the Kilimanjaro park gate. The climbers who were rock stars in descending disappeared, while I was struggling with my painful knees and toes. But I kept on walking with a heel toe marching drill that brought some relief. We were just a couple of hours away. I was very eager to get to the gate now. Samit was accompanying Ashir and me. He was having trouble with his knees as well.

It turned out that an elderly gentleman who was in his 70s and had made it to the top, was having trouble walking down. He was being rescued that day. I had seen the merry porters bouncing him down on the one-wheel stretcher. Our guide Nick devised a plan to get me to the gate a bit early. He asked the rescue van that was coming for the elderly gentleman to return for me. I broke the exciting news to Samit about a possible arrival of a rescue van that he could hop on. Finally just when we were a couple of kilometers away, the rescue-van that spoke perfect Mandarin while reversing, arrived on the scene. The driver was surprised to see a reasonably healthy female climber (yours truly) happily walking into the van. The rescue van is meant for people who arrive on one-wheel stretchers. Nick told him some cock and bull story in Swahili. I didn't know what he said, but I was sure that most of it was not true. The driver was a good soul and appeared to be satisfied with the explanation. A few yards ahead, we picked up Samit and Ashir. Samit's dream of an emergency evacuation was finally fulfilled.

The mood at the Kilimanjaro gate was festive. Porters and guides were singing the Kilimanjaro song, the cameras were working overtime and everyone was fist bumping after a very successful climb. Every returning climber has to sign out in the park's register. Having got that out of the way, we felt light and ready to hit a restaurant. Ananda even claimed that he had developed six packs. For a few seconds, the five men in our group crowded around him inspecting the packs. Ashwani summarily rejected Ananda's claim.

We now had food on our minds. But the guides will first take you to an overpriced shop of African artifacts intended to empty our pockets of US dollars. Everybody was yearning for spicy Indian food. Yes, Indians travel thousands of miles only to eat Indian food. We found an Indo-Italian restaurant, which I feared would be neither Indian nor Italian. But it did just fine except that it took the pole-pole philosophy much too seriously and served us food three hours after we ordered it.

The boys had already hatched a plan for an entire goat to be skewered and BBQed, African style. The only time Ashir takes an initiative is when there is a goat and a BBQ involved. He was entrusted with the job of organising a goat to be roasted for a celebratory dinner at the hotel, and all the guides and porters were invited. Ashir exhibited the same passion for the BBQed goat as Ronaldo has for a ball — the word 'inseparable' comes to mind. The rest of us had another task to complete.

We now needed to tip the guides and porters for their incredible work. The tipping ritual is an elaborate one and needs plenty of thought. Ananda took charge of the collection process, while the group volunteered me for the task of handing over the tip money to the head guide. The general pool of tip money was to be divided equally in a socialist style among all the porters and guides. Then, in a capitalist spirit, additional tip money was unequally allocated to the favored lot or our inner circle of guides. Those who had shown more allegiance to the Indian contingent (us) were tipped handsomely. The guide who carried Ananda's camera and took lots of photos was generously tipped by most of us. The climbers tipped the guides who helped them with their summit climb. Some guides who started to go beyond their call of duty a couple of days before the tipping day, even reminding me of their special services got lucky as well.

By 7:00 pm, the beer bottles were opened, and the mood among the partygoers was relaxed and happy. Then the goat was brought in amidst rousing cheers, and placed aesthetically on the table. It looked more like a toasted goat, skewered on a wooden poll that was thrust through the goat's rear, only to show up on the other side, out of its mouth. The head was still raw, with the white fur intact.

Disclaimer: The opinions about the goat in this book are purely personal.

In Chef Abbasi's supreme Picasso moment, he pulled out the wooden poll and thrust a bunch of leaves in the goat's mouth. The toasted goat appeared to be chewing on the leaves as it waited to be chewed upon by hungry Kilimanjaro climbers. We received our certificates, and some of us even made short speeches a la Academy Awards. The guides topped it all by teaching us the Kilimanjaro song as we danced to it.

Jambo! Jambo bwana!
Habari gani? Mzuri sana!
Wageni, mwakaribishwa!
Kilimanjaro? Hakuna matata!

While we were mulling over how the climb unfolded for each of us, and the life-lessons and experiences we were taking back with us, Samit was feeding pieces of the toasted goat to a hungry pregnant cat, and singing a popular Bollywood song 'Rocket Saiyyan', loosely translated as My Rocket Hubby.

***

Don't Miss the Forest

Mount Kilimanjaro taught me a thing or two about life. Sometimes it's important not to have a clear and specific idea about how far is your destination. The guides disclosed to us after we returned from the summit that they begin the final summit climb at night because if we could see how far we had to go, we would never go that far. In the dark, this becomes easier. The next step is the only thing that matters, regardless of what you are going after. You could be climbing a mountain or cleaning your garage or building a business.

What drives ordinary people like me to embark on an extraordinary journey? It's the lust for the unknown that excites us to pack our backpacks and head out. As we step out of our comfort zone, the possibilities beyond the seemingly impossible nourish our soul. Life's wonders as they unfold when we have a profound experience, give us the dopamine to continuously reinvent ourselves in subtle ways. Every minute, hundreds of ordinary souls in some part of the world are stepping out of their comfort zone with nervous anticipation.

Ordinary people can do with a little extraordinary in their lives.

You can have a personal motivation or a larger purpose. It doesn't matter what it is, but you must have one. Why are you climbing that mountain or going after a sales deal or learning a new programming language? It must be crystal clear in your head. Admittedly, we all lose sight of it in difficult times. But you have to keep reminding yourself whenever the chips are down. Even when I was delirious — in the darkest moments of that climb, the purpose was continuously processing in my head in an infinite loop.

You must enjoy the whole experience and want to do it again. This is what ordinary people do. Don't miss the forest for the trees. Karan loves to climb mountains because he loves being by himself and walking. The whole experience makes him a better human being. After all, life is a corpus of all our experiences. Ananda climbs mountains because it makes him feel accomplished and detached from life's pulls and pressures. For Samit, it was the thrill of doing something challenging. For me, it was my love for walking. When I walk, I feel life slowing down a little, letting me see it in all its magnificent colors — the good, the bad and the ugly. As a child, I wasn't much of an athlete. Let's just say I couldn't run to save my life. But I loved to walk. My dad always told me to walk with purpose, if I wanted a place in a world where men generally called the shots. He said, 'Walk like our Prime Minister, Indira Gandhi. She walks faster than her entire cabinet of ministers.' I also wanted to see what would it take for a woman with average stamina and physical strength to climb a mountain.

There is no way to be absolutely certain that we will all make it to our destination. There is no way to reverse engineer the perfect technique to get there. It's the confluence of so many factors that help us along the way that it is important to just enjoy the experience because in the end, we would never really be sure that it is our day to summit the mountain. But everyone will come away slightly wiser.

If anything, Mount Kilimanjaro teaches us the value of Pole Pole. There is no better way to handle the pressures of high altitude and scarce oxygen. This is why even a 70 year old can make it to the top, while plenty of youngsters who race up to the summit are bewildered at their inability to deal with high altitude. Africans have taught the world the enduring value of going slow and reflecting on life. What is the big rush? Nothing will ever get done a second before its time. When we don't get results quickly or find our expectations shortchanged, we should just think Pole Pole. Rumi famously said, 'It's rigged — everything, in your favor. So there is nothing to worry about.' Pole Pole was implicit in his optimism.

Ultimately, this is about teamwork, about how humans right from the Stone Age have come together to beat overwhelming odds. I learnt that collaboration is not merely a nice to have corporate agenda. Humans have used teamwork as a survival weapon against challenges of epic proportions. The climbers did little things for each other, shared what they had, waited for those who were straggling behind. Karan taught me how to hold my hiking poles so that I didn't strain my wrist. We all drew energy from each other. A little 'Come on Shalini' went a long way. A shared experience is far richer than opting for a journey alone with a guide and a porter. The guides and porters form a robust support system to take you there. So when we reach the summit or any destination for that matter, we need to dig a hole and bury our ego right there, and bring back just gratitude.

Nature challenges you, takes you to the edge, shows you your place in the universe, and lets you claw your way out of the abyss. During that process, you may give up several times. Your body may give up several times. But drag yourself up and keep going like the Phoenix, a mythical bird that is born again and again. It lives for hundreds of years and meets a fiery end, only to rise from its ashes. It's a beautiful legend of regeneration and endeavour. When I was faced with the moment of deepest despair, I had no idea that Stella Point was moments away. Had I given up at that point, I would have regretted not trying just a little bit harder.

Often, success is awaiting just a few steps beyond your moment of greatest despair.

When you get to the top, you realise how well nature has armed you with weapons like intuition, mindfulness, and motivation. In 1996, when Gary Kasparov played chess with IBM's super computer Deep Blue, he was able to outdo the machine whenever he was able to effectively use the irrational part of his brain. But in the middle of the game when the chess pieces have an inordinate number of possible moves, the super computer uses brute computational force to outdo the human. But at the start and the end of a chess game, when there are a limited number of moves, Gary would use intuition, gut feeling and creative thinking to plot his moves, which confused the computer. The computer had a certain amount of predictability and lacked the power of creative thinking. We have the power of the irrational to beat the odds in times of war, natural calamity or personal crisis.

Make no mistake. Like my mother said, 'There is no need to be extra *bahadur.*' It's okay to quit at any point. There is nothing wrong in giving up, to climb that mountain another time, or try something else. Don't risk it all to get to the top. But if you have an iota of hope that you could possibly make it, let that hope fester and surge into irrational energy that will carry you to the top, even though your body has all but broken down.

Keep walking Pole Pole.

Printed in Great Britain
by Amazon